This book is presented to:

Live the life! (p.7)
Doug.

Simplifying our lives:
Insights to living fully now

This book is part of the Insights Series. You may enjoy these other titles in this series, all by Douglas D. Germann, Sr.:

• Contraplanned: Contrarian insights on goal-setting, planning, and success
• Simplifying our lives: Insights to living fully now
• Leaping through flames: Insights for leaders
• Beyond Dollars and Numbers: Insights on business, work, and money
• Beyond creativity: Insights on daring, discovery and dreamsmithing
• How to get to happy from here: The happiness insights
• Everyday Awe: Insights to the divine at work and play

Also by Douglas D. Germann, Sr.:
• Buying a Business (For Very Little Cash)

Simplifying our lives:
Insights to living fully now

Douglas D. Germann, Sr.

Copyright © 1999, Learning Works, Incorporated. All rights reserved.

Learning Works, Incorporated
Mishawaka, Indiana, USA

SIMPLIFYING OUR LIVES: INSIGHTS TO LIVING FULLY NOW.
Copyright © 1999, Learning Works, Incorporated. All rights reserved. Printed in United States of America, and published at Mishawaka, Indiana. No part of this book may be used or reproduced in any manner whatsoever without advance written permission, except for brief quotations embodied in critical articles and reviews. For information, address Learning Works, Incorporated, 415 Lincoln Way West, Mishawaka, IN 46544. Telephone 219/255-0022, fax 219/255-0024, e-mail 76066.515@CompuServe.com.

First printing

Attention Organizations, Companies, Churches, Schools: Quantity discounts are available on bulk purchases of this book for educational purposes, fund raising, promotional, and award purposes. Special books or book excerpts can also be created to meet your specific needs. For information, please contact: Special People Department, Learning Works, Incorporated, 415 Lincoln Way West, Mishawaka, IN 46544. Telephone 219/255-0022. Fax 219/255-0024, e-mail 76066.515@CompuServe.com.

Library of Congress Catalog Card Number: 98-67264

ISBN 0-9665604-1-8

Contents

Introduction: Hints for getting ever-deeper insights from *Simplifying our lives*   1

The insights   3

Rounding out our lives   93

About the author   95

Special thanks to: 97

Order blank   99

For Linda

Introduction:
Hints for getting ever-deeper insights from *Simplifying our lives*

Thank you for buying the Insights Series. It is an investment in your long-term happiness.

Read this more slowly than most other books. Savor the words and the thoughts. This book is to be sipped, not guzzled.

Here are four ways or levels at which you can understand each insight. Try one after the other, or take them in any order. One session could contain more than one level. When one insight catches your mind, try one or more of these steps with it. Probably you will only read four or five insights at a sitting.

A. Surface: a literal reading of the insight.

B. Get personal: practice, apply it to your life. Test it out. See what it does in your life. See how you might like to vary it. Find the part in it that says to you, "This is about me!"

C. Symbolical: look for the part that has double meaning for you. The vast majority of the insights have at least double meaning. Soon you may be seeing triple meanings or more.

D. Resting and unitive: sometimes you'll reach a place where you say "Yes!" The insight seems to be something you could have said: You utter it and it utters you. You rest in it and just let it soak in and become part of you.

You can find more value in these insights. Seek ways to make them yours. Mark them. Chew on them. Read them just before you go to sleep and just when you get up to prime your unconscious and conscious. Make the insights a part of your life and they can help you change your life.

Warning: If you cannot find something here from which your life, heart or business can prosper, then it is a signal you're not truly awake.

These are discoveries made in the experiment, discoveries that can lead you to your own more significant truths. Look for your own meanings. Your life is full of meaning—you need only look around. My role is to help you notice. Look and see.

The Insights Series and *Simplifying our lives* is as much by you and about you as it is by and about me. You are on every page, if you have eyes to see. Mine your own insights as you go. Record your own insights before they fly away free, so many butterflies of beauty and wonder now gone.

You will find some of these insights pretty surface level, some will remind you of old things, some surprising. This is a book to re-read, to come back to again and again to mine more from the same shaft.

Doug

The Insights

- Please don't read this book. Do this book. Use it.

- Everything in this life may not have a purpose, yet it fills one.

- Life is not a straight line experience. Life is a divergent puzzle, with many solutions. This is the chaos, the deeper order, the meaning of life.

- The interruption is the main event.

- Can we give ourselves good gifts, like time each day with no purpose?

- We need a time to attend to our loftiest thoughts, to climb the mountain and get a broader view, even to enjoy. We need like food the nourishment of seeing beyond our daily blindness.

- We can instantly choose to change.

- Life at its base is a mystery. Awe is a very good response. Sometimes it is the only proper response.

- What are you doing now that will make you unafraid to die when the time comes? Are you living your legacy? Will you be able to say that you actually did live?

- We need to become completely transparent, so that the world can see us for all we are. So that we can see us for all we are. So we can see we are good.

- What is practical about all this? Healing is aided. Creativity. Courage. Hope. Love. Cooperation. Improvement. Trying again. Trying in spite of. Trying the first time.

- We are the emptiness, the lack-of-gift, the need of gift.

- We don't want to go where we need to go; we want to go where we will want to go.

Douglas D. Germann, Sr.

- I don't have to get to the depths every time—just be present. It would be boring and probably harmful to always see the profound.

- All humans illustrate with their lives how they think a life should be led—at least at the time. And each time, all the time. More exactly, we're trying to find how a life should be led.

- You are not just you. You are part of the community, family, nation, world, universe, creation. We must learn to get in tune with this fact, to feel appropriately small and large at the same time, to be connected. "You are more than you are." It is a statement and a puzzle.

- Learn what works.

- What is a life? How is it built, how experienced? Or, is it imposed upon us from without? What makes it good or bad?

- Shrink not from life.

- Life is movement. Therefore life is constant transition: a wave form. In this sense, we are each a human becoming.

- Do not doubt the worthiness of the gift you are given to carry to the people.

- For many people what they early thought was their special weakness turned out to be their biggest strength, their spiritual gift.

- We as humans have the gift of striving, of knowing our potential is always beyond our grasp. This should not be frustrating. It can be something from which we drink deeply and breathe fully and from which we move out hopefully.

- Why should we look at life expectantly when it has been giving us nothing but hard times recently? In part so we can remind ourselves that there is more to come, "after these messages...."

- Living is an art with infinite possibilities.

Douglas D. Germann, Sr.

◆ Live the life you were invited here to live.

- So much of our lives is spent at a surface, superficial level. When will we get real?

- Some gifts are created, realized, unwrapped, released by our accepting them. Even when we don't want them or fear them.

- How do you know who you are unless you slow down long enough to find out?

- How many directions are there? How about these? North, South, East, West, Up, Down, Inside, Outside, Openness, Closedness. Can you point out the others?

- Fear does get in the way of love. I've seen this the last few days with the attempted intimidation by an IRS agent. Is fear the opposite, an opposite, or an opposer of love?

- We have it backwards—we seek connection by trying to separate ourselves, trying to stand out from the crowd.

- Attitude is the same as human spirit.

Douglas D. Germann, Sr.

- So far as I can think, we're the only animal which scratches each others' backs.

- My weak understanding changes daily. Today it is that the more fully alive others are, the more enjoyment for all of us. New things forever emerge to challenge us to be fully alive, fully awake. We are all one so we want every fiber of our being to enjoy, be awake and alive, for its own sake: joy gives us joy.

- Sentimental is still mental.

- There is value on both sides of the coin: wisdom and ignorance; strength and vulnerability; age and youth.

- Be bold in life, timid in little.

- Think you, because you can eat our food, you know us? You are barely scratching the surface. Come, get to know us....

- The world doesn't have to stop for us to get off.

- You are your own bridge between living and living fully, which you must travel yourself.

- We have an innate fear of death and of the worthlessness of our lives. Therefore, we want something to live beyond us, to say to ourselves that this life was not wasted. Children help fulfill this need on a surface level. But we want deeper than this to know we have mattered. This is natural, in-built. But from where does this desire arise? It is part and parcel of our deepest being. Why? What put it there? We want instinctively to live longer than we are given. Do we suspect that we do? Is the desire proof of its fulfillment?

-

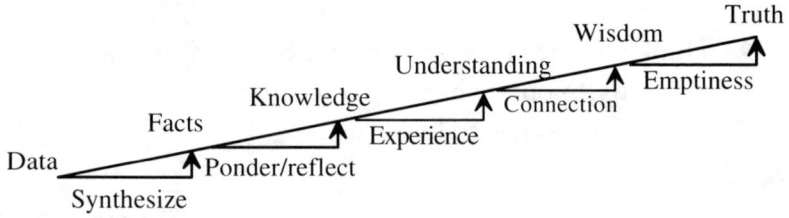

- Reason will tell you we're all separate; experience tells you we're all one. Both can be correct at once.

- The doctor can tap my knee and make my foot kick, and I can use my other hand to move my little finger, even though the tendon is severed and it cannot move on its own. In the same way, we can excite parts of the brain with electrical impulses and thereby project old memories or certain actions or thoughts. But without the intentionality, the motivating force behind them, they are meaningless. We still don't know what or "where" the mind is.

- We are only living half-lives if we ignore spirit.

- We need to be vigilant to rid ourselves of platitudes and instead to engage, encounter, touch something deep inside that flows through us...and others...and all.

- To leave your legacy purposefully, you must first perceive what you have to give: perhaps even make an inventory.

Simplifying our lives

- Parks are necessary to life. This greenery provides a habitat for trees and plants to replenish our oxygen, and animals to make the circle of life complete. Their quietness makes us complete.

- I have often wondered how humankind looks to God. Being outside of time, a person and the child and grandchild and parent and grandparent must all appear as parts of one endless necklace, all flowing out of each other, all parts of each other.

- My business is death. If you consider the odds are that you will someday die, it is your business, too.

- Purposeless living—there is perhaps as much or more good there as in living on purpose.

- Do we not want to go beyond balance to transcending both personal and impersonal, while including them?

- Flowers may wilt and dry, but beauty lasts.

Douglas D. Germann, Sr.

- What are the most powerful matters in your life? Should you maybe pay more attention to them?

- Life is a fathomless enigma, a 3-D puzzle with uncountable pieces, a mystery simple but huge. Still, life is good.

- Today, time is running faster than I am. Which is right? Could it be I?

- A baby does something just by being—brings love to the world. Notice that it is passive—the child brings love by merely accepting it.

- The inspired life comes when you remain alert every moment to the lessons.

- We know all there is to know, though we don't know it all. There it is deep within us, yet we need to learn to listen, explore, and be reminded.

- There is nothing outside of you which can hurt you.

Simplifying our lives

- Fingers warm faster on warmer body parts than clasped tightly to their own cold. Yet we tend to only hold them to themselves.

- Have we perhaps diverted our original pioneer spirit and the rugged individualism that grew out of it, into a modern day hermitism? We hide in our electronic cocoons, afraid to touch each other, in ways that the earliest people in the new world would have found strange. They came to freely practice religion, a group activity. Their strongest image is the Thanksgiving feast, a get-together. Separation is bad for us.

- You cannot possibly be aware of all your surroundings. What then? You can at least choose to be aware of some. Too often we are not aware of any of them, moving from here to there, only paying attention to what we imagine will be there and then, or was here and then, and so we actually miss the here and now.

- Look. See.

- The nightly news is less important than we think. It fulfills a basic human drive to gossip and more deeply to care for each other. It enables us to respond to others' needs because we know of those needs. It gives us an entry into connection because it shows us what is probably on our peers' minds. But it can also interfere with our ability to go deeper in conversation and thought, and with our peace of mind, and with our use of time for more important things. Here is a place where we need a balance, but we need only a drop on the news side of the scale: a taste, not a whole meal, nor even a bite.

- These are the best years of our lives!

- We not only inherit from our elders, but from our own childhood.

- My anger is not to be fought but to be loved away, since anger is often a partial lack of compassion.

- Is it possible to silence the chattering of our minds to hear what is out there, and still live?

Simplifying our lives

- We are a three-dimensional jigsaw puzzle: all extremely individual, but not complete till part of the whole.

- We are held in place by gossamer Lilliputian threads. Eventually there are so many we think we cannot get loose. But if we break one now, cut one later, eventually twos and threes and groups can be severed, and we can be free to be the giants we are.

- We need to move toward a deeper experience of life and the divine.

- To awaken, you sometimes first have to go to sleep.

- The negativity of the "bad guys" is in us, and not out there.

- Life to life, eye to eye, depth to depth: how we should communicate.

- Solitude is basic: a time each day to re-collect, reflect, and clarify.

◆ One of the biggest secrets of this world is that everyone is always going through transition.

- The reason Grandmas are so persuasive is that they get inside you. They see from your side.

- The future can change the past.

- Our middle years are our power years.

- In connectedness is infinite power, freedom, and happiness; and pain, tears, weakness, sweat.

- All you ever have to be is you in all your uniqueness and wholeness. That is all you ever can be. Everything else is fraud. Embrace your self, not your fraud.

- There are two kinds of I, and they arise from what we use the other to refer to. If our I refers to It, then it makes us into an it, an object. If to You, then it makes us into a person.

- Start thinking of the body as a physical manifestation of fields of meaning and processes of information.

◆
>   Life is my love:
>   Love is my life.
>   Is life my love?
>   Is love my life?
>   Love my life is:
>   Life my love is.
>   Love is life, my!
>   Life is love, my!

◆ See the caterpillar, how she changes over and over.

◆ Prepare not for leaner times, but for abundance. Realize abundance may be beyond the areas of your previous experience or preconceived notions: be ready, open your eyes, there it is!

◆ Be gently real.

◆ We are all holograms of the universe, including all parts: earth, air, fire, water, plants, animals, humans, mind. You and I are one, yet different!

◆ Is awe an emotion?

- We need to move beyond the compulsive to the higher impulse.

- Our lives are a three-dimensional web which we are both discovering and creating. This web is itself within the larger 3-D web of the universe and life itself, which all of us are again constantly discovering and creating. This is a piece of the energy that propels the universe.

- One in all, all in one.

- Life is like paddling a canoe in a river. We affect the river, the river affects us. There are random rocks and eddies, vees and pillows. When we go with the current, power is not necessary at all times to keep progressing—just for steering. But we still make mistakes and miscalculations. May you be with the force.

- Life is ever in the balance.

- Get a life—you can create any life you like.

- Are you loverly? Do you make an effort to be a good lover?

- What is it that helps us recognize someone we haven't seen in years, whose face and whole body have changed? Even if we're not sure at first—in moments we know, It is the person's spirit. What is it that we remember of our deceased loved ones? Certainly not their accumulations or awards, but their personality, their soul, their spirit. Yet spirit does not equal personality.

- All life is a transforming process.

- He is in the chocolate,
    She is in the shell,
    Here, it's in the fruit chews,
    And salty nut as well.

- Re-turning leads us home.

- Love is primarily an action, not a feeling.

- It's time we got our lives off dead circumference. We need to truly start living from the center.

- It is a mystery that we are most free when we are hooked up!

- We humans crave the wide open road and a place to lay our heads. Strange.

- When you reach the point where you painfully realize your life is not working, that something is dreadfully wrong, this is good. You have reached a launching point: from here you can stay on the road you don't like knowing it won't be good for you, or you can set off on a new one.

- Wouldn't it be useful in our society if we put up road signs reading, "Speed trap ahead"?

- Life begins to make sense when you give spirit its place.

- Why are names for our diseases reassuring? Because then we think we have control over them.

- We long for true life where we can see the meaning, be the meaning, create the meaning, stand in and be carried away by the current of spirit, wave and energy.

- We are more seekers than holders of the truth, the real. Yet we cannot escape the real. If we look ahead, there it looms. If we look behind, there it is. And on each side it walks with us.

- I'm not sure whether I'm confused, or befuddled.

- Breathing includes life and death. Breathing is a small rehearsal of life cycles: every inspiration a receiving of life, every expiration a giving it back, every pause in between a waiting on the external, the beyond.

- Beauty and truth and love and goodness are what lasts. Pick the good part.

Simplifying our lives

- What is the opposite of spirit? It is dullness, sleep, unconscious, not being present, not absorbing.

- The key technique in connecting and re-connecting with the people in our lives is to try, to experiment. Like a good back rub, where you don't do the same motion over and over but try to vary as much as possible, to invent, to make all life an adventure!

- The modern *1984* would not have a Big Brother, but a more insidious group of obsequious servants to whom we had turned over, unseeing, all our freedoms, little by little. Servants like TVs, microwaves, computers. One day we awaken (hopefully) to see ourselves enslaved to our servants, unable to live for ourselves.

- Without you it all collapses.

- There is perhaps a connecting place between doing and being, where "just" being is not letting the moment go unnoticed, and therefore unused.

- Shh! Listen. Shh.

- Until the law gets beyond its reliance only on logic, it will never be fair. Logic cannot know justice: justice includes mercy. That's why justice is unknown to the law.

- At many deep levels we are all connected. We are made of the same atoms. We have the same emotional energy. Radio waves pass through us and winds pass around us all the same. We all walk on the same earth. In fact we share the basic electrons with the ground. We are part of the same quantum physics field. We are one.

- Winter and Spring are doing battle. Today belligerent Winter is throwing an offensive at mild Spring. Our towns and our homes and our very lives are the battleground. Yet we know which will win. Winter can only defeat doddering old Autumn.

- Because of the raw spot within, we are afraid to open it to others. Yet that is the pulsing place from which real connection comes.

- As a child, I learned that mazes were more easily solved by working backwards from the goal. Perhaps it might be worth a try with life.

- The reason Grandpas are so loved is that they have a *laissez faire* attitude—"let the kid be a kid"—and he is a kid with them!

- We are a synthesis of what our parents tried to teach and accomplish. We also bring to life our own experiences and our mind. These all work together to create new insights. All of these we integrate into something new. We are both integrators of the past and creators of the future. We are endowed with the ability to pause, think, and then do something entirely new and outside the trajectories of the past!

- In stillness is power.

- What is lightweight? What is the weight of light? It is actually heavy, dense, piercing, hard to hide, substantial.

- Ask yourself, "what is the important stuff in my life?" Dig beneath the surface answers.

- With all those neurotransmitters firing all the time, how can we call our mind undisciplined, especially that part connected to the brain? How can we hope to discipline it?

- A moment is a point in time and also outside of time. It is of indefinite time and infinite time. It is the meeting of time and eternity. In it, we can begin to hold eternity in our hands, in an instant, for an instant. There are infinite numbers of points in time as there are infinite numbers of points on a line.

- Are you using and giving your all?

- In order to feel the tenderest touch on the web of our being, we need to sensitize ourselves to it. Practice and learn. Look through your eyes and through the reflections to what is really there.

- Forgiving others for their separations from us involves also forgiving ourselves for willingly being drawn to the mirage that we are separate.

- We can't give it all away.

- There is a justice trap: It's not just that life is not fair, it's also that we cannot and should not look for a cheap way out: someone else to bail us out.

- Compulsions focus on getting, grasping, accumulating. Impulses focus on something coming from deep within and deep without which lead us to giving, letting go, letting flow. One tries to dam the stream, the other to go with it. At each moment and from moment to moment, we choose. The stream itself is our true self, our freedom to reach toward home.

- We are islands in life's waters, looking and acting separate, yet part of the same earth.

Simplifying our lives

- This is my prime.

- It is necessary for us to live on the surface of the earth so we can have the optimal temperature, atmosphere, food. Yet we are also refreshed and need the crisp air and stars above and the cool water from deep.

- Parents teach what is necessary for their children to live in this world; grandparents go beyond and teach unconditional love.

- If the mind is solely in a mechanical brain, how can we not get something to "sink in?" Like when my wife told me both my parents had died within minutes of each other of separate heart attacks, I incredulously blurted, "You're k..." and caught myself. Why do we even have to have a word, incredulous? A computer would take the new data without questioning it and base its new decisions and actions on the new information. Humans are not so constricted.

- Life is an experience—don't miss it!

- Roots also are a metaphor for connection, always seeking more depth, more moisture, more nutrients.

- Breaking bread together is a way of saying (usually unconsciously) we're taking into ourselves the same thing, our bodies are at this time made of the same thing, we are more one than separate. We are, after all, what we eat.

- Go out of your head—into your heart.

- We are one. We don't just have similarities: there is a vibrant orange and green thread which runs through us all. It can be snapped and made thinner—but it remains connected and can grow and be made thicker so that we become perfectly one, as Jesus prayed.

- We are separate and we are one, both at the same time—at least in the scientific sense that we are all energy—if not in the metaphysical sense. Peace comes as we concentrate more effort on looking for and seeing the oneness.

Simplifying our lives

- Reason and even wisdom are mirrors through which we see ourselves: we do not see beyond. Mereness is mirrorness.

- When we give our gift away, it expands.

- We need to move from synchronicity (doing something at the same time) to identity, knowing we are one.

- Neither trees nor roots can live without the other. If one rots, or roots into poor soil or water or air, the whole dies. But the roots come first.

- Those screwy, offensive drivers are just expressing another part of me which I choose not to express—the me that is local and the me that is universal. Therefore, I can let them do their thing and through them express what I choose not to express.

- Pay attention to the *obiter dicta*.

- Do not be dismayed by transient things.

- Do not look at your watch while traveling. It can only increase your anxiety and preoccupation, not in any appreciable way your speed or progress. Looking puts you out of touch with what is going on around you. Besides being dangerous, you miss the riches.

- Slow up ↑!

- There is undeniably more to life than what we can know. If we can imagine it, it is possible. Yet we can imagine more than our logic can comprehend. This is testimony that there is more than we can understand. Knowledge goes beyond understanding. Reality goes beyond knowledge.

- What difference does it make whether the music comes from within me or without? It is all in the universe, part of the universe, the universe flows through it all; I am part of the universe, and am of equal dignity with it. It is all real, all truth. Therefore, what is without is within, and what is within is without, if I allow it.

Simplifying our lives

- We perish or flourish: there is no balance.

- What accounts for the difference between wisdom and aging? Attention.

- I am bigger than this little case called the body. My mind is larger and roams wider than from ear to ear. My spirit touches and is touched by others I only read about. This I know without need of proof.

- Are you good and getting better?

- At the least, we are one in being.

- A client, after years of struggling with a daughter run amok, finally left her nothing in his Will and trust. However, he did leave a good gift to his daughter, a gift it took a lot of guts to make: a wake up call. Truth is, we all get wake up calls everyday, and many of us have stopped listening. We always have the opportunity to listen again.

- Just be.

- Have patience with your impatience.

- Being more human is more effective.

- If life goes on, then we must of necessity be on a path which never ends, constantly improving, creating, arriving, departing, changing, seeing new.

- Freedom includes, captivity excludes. The free person has all choices open, the captive has had some foreclosed.

- Deeper *is* higher:

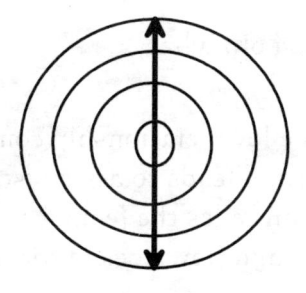

- Your weakness may actually be your strength.

Simplifying our lives

- Sometimes our lack of faith is unreasonable. This morning I had to get up at 3:50 for a flight. After tossing for some time, I got up and looked at the time—3:28. Despite two alarms being set, I lacked faith in them. Perhaps there are also times when it is unreasonable to not have faith in the future, God, whatever we doubt.

- We need wonder: wonder—wow!; and wonder if I took the right turn.

- Life is a game. A few rules you discover in the play. Mostly you make your own rules. And they will be different rules each round.

- We feel the tug of...what?

- Sometimes the love relationship comes from the feeling and leads to action, sometimes the action precedes the feeling and relationship. It's ebb and flow, locked together.

- Ask constantly, Is this a raisin in my gruel?

- Don't say nothing: avoid "interesting," "nice," "fine." Be gutsy: say something.

- Each of us is in the world, the web of life, the universe. The world, web and universe would not be exactly the same without us. Therefore, we are the world, web and universe.

- Seen from a distance, an atom is an indivisible whole. Yet it is made up of whirling electrons, quarks, and all manner of substantial and insubstantial things. So too much of this life.

- If Superman were really super, he'd do quantum leaps and not go whooshing through intermediate space.

- Why can't/don't men wear ribbons and flowers in their hair?

- Fear comes from the head level, love comes from the soul level.

- How wide and deep is your spirit!

Simplifying our lives

- I'm beginning to believe that the key to getting along with one another is a conscious realization that at base we are connected. Anger at other drivers stems from seeing them as separate from us—when we see we are one, each as part of the human comedy, we can smile and make allowances. Teen gangs are ways to connect and say "I'm important, I'm one of the important people."

- Encourage yourself to do what you think good; discourage yourself from the bad.

- It is spring and the evergreens have ten million soft green fingers, each tipped with a golden thimble.

- When your actions and your own big picture are in harmony you will have peace and power.

- Perhaps chaos does not exist, except in confusion of mind.

- We are permeated with the universe: where does the universe end and we begin?

Douglas D. Germann, Sr.

◆ Sometimes things seem meaningless simply because we cannot understand. That doesn't mean they have no meaning.

- If we think back over our stories, and play with them and let them run with us, we may find we are able to change the past.

- We have faculties which we can, if we wish the benefits, arrange to work in a team: our will, experience, imagination, memory, spirit, emotion, reason, well of inexhaustible resources. One alone cannot do the job of the whole crew.

- We are not so much a two-part self, higher and lower. We rather have dispersed aspects of ourselves on a continuum, some for a time higher than others. We never know how high the high may be, how low the low. Our job is to reunite our pieces, not so much in a high place on the spectrum, but pointed higher, moving higher. In that directional movement is in fact the highest point.

- We blast the bad guys in our movies and video games—vaporize them. In real life the bad guys are a part of us and don't disappear—become good—until we love them.

- Why do we spend money on medical care for the elderly? Hope. Hope that we can restore their vitality. This hope is beyond reason and shows us there is something real beyond reason.

- Sex and death are two sides of the same coin.

- A man who has found his feminine, nurturing, compassionate side is whole as God is whole: he sees both the hard and the soft. The same may be said of a woman who has found her masculine side.

- Life is little bubbles, melting into each other.

- One point of my folks' death is their very mode of death (both died within minutes of each other of separate heart attacks) was a gift. Although we cannot all make a statement by how we die, we can still make the statement. But more deeply, we can and do make our gifts by how we live, by the examples from (not of—lest we feel guilty) our lives. We learn by anecdotes first, then make principles.

Simplifying our lives

- What do bubbles and hot air balloons and other floating, flying things symbolize to us? That we are free? That part of us wants to fly away? That our body recognizes its own spirit?

- What is sound tends to resonate.

- Race is an obvious difference between people. Yet most agree it is but a surface distinction, and therefore not a logical, just or right basis for decisions. This is just an inkling of why it is good to go beneath the surface, and of the fact that we are really all alike deep down where it counts.

- Life is not foolproof.

- In this country we are uniquely advantaged by way of having so many associations, which allow us to create virtual organizations and ubiquitous learning by networking and our know-how in adult learning.

- If death does not make any sense, how can life?

- Being good, doing good is not enough. We must be whole. Then we learn good is part of the whole. We are no longer acting to earn a prize. Good flows naturally, uncontainably.

- I am superb. Actually, I am magnificent.

- Is it the tangible versus the intangible, or are they each part of a whole? The intangible is just as necessary as the tangible, and not more so.

- The belief that there is something more to life is freeing, energizing. It confers power. It enhances life. It causes us to resonate.

- A + D = Danger. Anger plus demonstration leads to danger. A + C = Connection. Anger plus change can lead us to the other person.

- We want to act with integrity, to be integral, to be one, whole.

- From the quiet inside wells up light.

Simplifying our lives

- Ever notice that our words for the good guys—allies, solidarity, union—often convey a meaning of connection? By nature, we equate connection and good.

- Blurt the truth, study forth a lie. Delay is thought, gloss, time to prevaricate, construct, clean up, make pretty, acceptable. What comes first to mind has a better chance of being true.

- Control is an effort to separate us from the object (person or otherwise) we wish to control.

- When we pull back to observe our impulses, we are in a position to tell which are good and desirable.

- The human spirit is user-friendly, but only if you flip the On switch first.

- We must hold our hands and arms open so we can receive what is raining down on us—rather than grasping for fear of losing the little we already have.

Douglas D. Germann, Sr.

- The steering wheel does not steer. For that it requires an outside force: us. It is a tool. It goes round and round and does not care whether it comes back to the same place, goes beyond or stops short. So our life here.

- What is the nature of a gift? It is given without price, free. Yet it can be lost by rejection, by ignorance, by indifference.

- My wife, before we became engaged, on shopping for a wedding ring: "I don't know if I'd regret it for the rest of my life if I didn't get that ring." What would I have regretted if I didn't get that one? What would you regret not doing?

- We are the conduit for the gift.

- Sign for a bathroom door: "Disposed" (as in "She's in Disposed").

- The soft, the gentle, the simple, the love is stronger than anything negative or bad.

Simplifying our lives

- Connection is the opposite side of the coin of alienation, so talked-about in the 60's.

- Move beyond the surface reality. Real beauty is deeper than the skin.

- Ask always: What is this? What is this? Observe....

- We are like the fingers of our hand: We can act separately, we each have the illusion of separateness, yet we are all attached together and part of one.

- I possess wisdom, but I do not always or often apprehend it. So then I cannot put it to use. I should not try to grasp it or hang on to it.

- Important stuff just I.S.

- Consultants and writers tell you to indulge yourself while grieving—be kind to yourself. That is good. But it can be overdone. You can get to where you are less than indulgent of others, even intolerant.

Douglas D. Germann, Sr.

- Do I know what all I've written means? I cannot: each person brings his and her own meaning to it. Therefore I need to get it out, give freedom to its power.

- Sometimes I'm not ready to go to the depths: what I need to handle is closer to the surface. Sometimes a bird is just a bird.

- We already know it all (but we still need reminders).

- A wave never splashes far from the sea.

- For some it may be said, their lord is lard.

- It's not a matter of risk, it is immersing yourself in life.

- I am come today not to bring answers but questions. Questions which I cannot answer: questions which only you can answer. I do not even have all the questions.

- Live your dreams!

- There is more to life than what the first five senses tell us.

- Specks in our eyes are examples of defects we must learn to ignore.

- To be conscious is necessary: to be rational is not.

- Even if the stream seems to separate us, under the stream we connect, we are one humus.

- To get the value out of life, you must be present—to yourself, others, the sacred.

- Life is a daily thing. We are only given as much as we can handle. We need to see the extraordinary in the daily or it never exists. We bring something into existence by seeing it.

- Anger is a wound in need of healing.

- How do you do a mundane task, e. g. go to the grocery, drive a car, buy clothes? Pay attention. What does this say about your way of living? Your spirit wants out, will out.

Douglas D. Germann, Sr.

Simplifying our lives

- None of us knows the answers, yet each of us knows our answer. And that we know only partly. And we revel in what we don't know as much as what we do.

- Worry comes from not having done anything about whatever worries us. Doing something may be work toward solving or reducing the problem. It might be turning it over to another, maybe God. It means mostly doing something to reduce the worry to the point where we can control the thing... or not.

- Our personal universe expands as we move inward.

- We all live an interior life, and it is upon this that we build.

- Put more life in your life.

- Anger is my friend. Anger tells me what I should know. Anger is my friend.

- Curious. Love is not emotion, love is not logic. It is bigger than both, it encompasses both; it is both. Curious. How can something both be and not be something else?

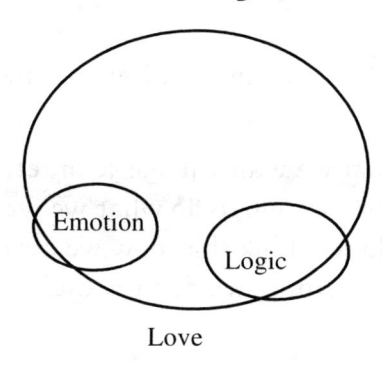

Diagram: a large oval containing two smaller overlapping ovals labeled "Emotion" and "Logic"; the large oval is labeled "Love".

- Try driving today with the radio off. Better yet, walk somewhere instead of driving.

- We go crazy if we try to stay in our own heads, communicate only with ourselves. We need interaction.

- Where in today's world are we bound and where free?

- If we turn away and cover our wounds, they cannot be tended and healed.

- Some people hold that on death we come back to earth in another form, time after time. What if we could live multiple lives all at once?

- Of course I'm changing! I'm growing.

- Why must we wait till age 50 or retirement or any future time to do what we want to do? Why do we think that now we are constricted to something we don't want?

- The Greek word for fate, *moira,* means portion or share: Fate has only a small part to say about our lives. It derives from the word *mer* which means to ponder—we have to ponder the part which does not fit, which comes from elsewhere and does not fit in. This opposes the part which flows from our choices and actions.

- Be overwhelmed by the light inside you.

- Seek deeper freedoms. Exercise deeper freedoms.

- You think, believe, feel and spiritually experience. Are you in touch with each, and how to use all four?

- Three ways to see: there is a part of us which can see the fingers as separate, a part which can see it as part of the hand, and a part which can see both.

- Why do we number the years? What are we counting towards? Or from? Are we counting like prisoners the days of our sentence? The years till we die? Taking the roll of the past? Why do we care to differentiate one year from the next?

- We are fragments of the whole puzzle, with parts which fill out the whole and with pieces missing. Others have different pieces missing but different pieces to complete us. Remembering this will help us have compassion for others.

- God's dream is holographic: even if it is shattered, it is all there in each shard—just more of it.

- Life is aquiver...with life!

- Ritual starts as a way to remind us where we are, who we are, and ends as ceremony. Thus, it must be renewed, turned back, constantly, vigilantly.

- Life is a process of becoming ever more conscious.

- What you have is enough. Who you are is enough.

- I must stand up boldly and in truth for the need for depth and silence; it is not for me to determine outcomes, or even to strive for them, just do my job.

- Everyone is dying for human contact. Let's help more get it before then.

- There is one person irreplacable—you. There is no duplicate.

- Coincidences are meaningful when we choose to see meaning in them.

- A Will is a dream for your family.

- Sometimes people around us may not be able to hear the message: it may be our job to help them hear.

- Spirit is where attitude comes from. Spirit stifled and we become bitter in outlook, timid in attitude. Spirit free we become bold, happy, soaring.

- In the past we were reminded that everybody had within them certain resources and resiliencies. Today, we think they are reserved for the rich, smart, elite, those who bought the tapes.

- We don't have time to be petty, nor is it good for our species if one of us holds back in the slightest any of the others.

- Soul equals self, but spirit goes even deeper inside to where you are connected to something bigger than yourself, to others.

- Everyone is on a journey and often we realize it. And often we just don't know what to do with it. So we do nothing.

- Open your eyes and talk.

- What I teach you already know. Better, I draw your attention to what you know and show you how easy it is to use, and how effective. Using the unused is better than starting the new.

- We are all the same. We are all one. Raising one raises all.

- The alarm clock is a way of cutting short our sleep, getting less than we need. Figure out the amount you need, then get to sleep in time.

- If you knew you were going to die on the way home, would you need to use the phone? Using the phone (now) like that is your legacy.

- Write about something ordinary.

Douglas D. Germann, Sr.

- The other day I listened to a man who used a lot of $1 and $5 words. Then he used a few I could not afford.

- We are, each of us, holograms of the divine. We were broken off in the big bang of creation, and carry with us the whole, the divine.

- What is spirit? That element, that energy that infuses and unites the whole universe. It is the sacred, the holy. It is the incorporeal but nonetheless real part of us and all about us. It is not physical, but it is in the physical. It is, for instance, in learning. It is awe, the sacred, the holy, wonder.

- The way to a man's heart attack is through his stomach.

- The real you is woven throughout your body, mind, soul, and spirit, inseparable, part of a whole. You cannot be dissected and remain you. There is an essence that suffuses and runs through you and is apparent to all who would see. It is this essence we see in the child undeveloped, the old person falling apart, and in the spirit when we meet again, after life.

- Life is not a balancing act.

- Love is not earned. Love is not counted by quantity. Love is not an emotion.

- What does your impending death say about your life?

- We are all wired to one source for energy; what we do with that energy is up to each of us.

- We have text, context, connotation; we wish to avoid pretext.

- We don't have to connect with spirit, just get out of the way.

- If you get yourself wrapped in too tight a package it might be difficult to unwrap from the inside.

- When we come to truth we don't know all there is to know, just what is important.

- What does it mean to us, "This is what I'm supposed to do"?

Simplifying our lives

- We know what survival is, but do we know living?

- A key to depth is in inner participation.

- Do what pleases you.

- Some people hatch out of their bubbles earlier than others, some never, and all can go back in when needed. Our bubbles are there to play with, to help us start flying, to protect us, and allow us to bounce. What is your bubble?

- Are we confused, or merely mystified?

- Don't just see yourself in others, discover yourself in them, through them.

- There is a power in healing intent and in human intent. It is brought to fruition by human touch.

- One first step in connecting is to first identify to what or whom you wish to connect, and then why.

- Sometimes we want to stay in the shallows. Perhaps it is easier. Perhaps it avoids the pain or the work. Perhaps it can get us easily or more quickly to a different place to enter the deeper water.

- Life is transitory. Yet there is a permanence behind it. Live in the transitory with the freedom of permanence. Live in permanence with the power of the transitory.

- Try praying: "I am willing."

- In anger, I feel your separation too, react to it, see it.

- How can we move from an agitated mind to calm? Rest, ask, release, loosen, shift.

- Three aspects of this subject: *praktikos*, practice; *theoria*, understanding; *logos*, experience of the word.

- It is a fantastically different kind of life you can have when you freely put Spirit first.

Simplifying our lives

- Once we are free-floating like a gyroscope, we can maintain our direction in spite of how upside down our world might get. It is a matter of wholeness, not balance.

- There are forces which pull us apart and forces which pull us together. Even that statement pulls us apart—unless we realize that those trying to pull apart are trying to express their individuality, uniqueness, separateness...their spirit. Then all *is* one.

- The difference between a man and a woman is that he takes things off his face in the morning and she puts things on—and each thinks they look better for it.

- Keepgiving is a term which means the action of giving something away and finding that we get more of the same back, like smiles.

- We probably ask all questions in relation to something else. "Does s/he love me?" means "Am I worthy?" or perhaps...well I can't think of anything else that doesn't resolve itself into this same question.

- Let your humanity show.

- I used to laugh that people went to "see" their Doctor. Perhaps to save expense they can merely park outside his or her office and look as he or she gets into the car and drives off! Seeing alone does not heal. Ah, but being seen can.

- Live deeply!

- You can't be beyond without being within. Without something to be beyond, there is no beyond.

- God will not be pinned down: I cannot pin myself down, then. I too am a mystery. Even to myself.

- If we go out and take a look at our world from space, we can begin to see that it is all contained in this place where we are alive this moment. We contain the universe in each molecule of ourselves.

Simplifying our lives

- Everyone is average, which means genius.

- As we move back to ultimacies all converges, like a reversal of the big bang. Doing right becomes truth, truth becomes love. The distinctions blur. All become the same:

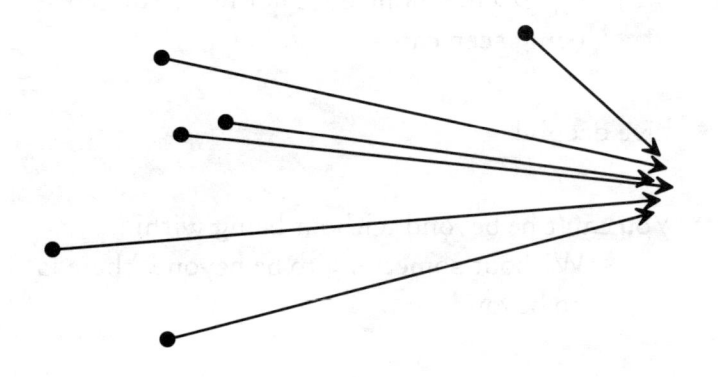

- In the last few weeks I have seen a couple billboards go up around town showing people with their arms thrown back in a gesture of exuberance. But in each case, one a man, one a woman, their hands were fists. The person they each depicted, with whom the public was meant to identify, was reserving something. Don't reserve! Extend!

- I have decided to eat less healthfully: eat less, and do it more healthfully.

- Do it anyway.

- How do we connect? Through touch. Through voice. Through attitude. Through glance. Through glands. Through hearing. Through presence. Through smell. Through spirits.

- The only thing we can say about us and the universe is how we relate one to the other. We love, hate, are personal, impersonal. Nothing is known of itself by itself. Even quantum physics is today talking of observer participancy: neither the observer nor the observed exists without the other. Life is truly in the in-betweens. All is dynamics.

- What is the good life?

- Sometimes we are purely in the physical world, sometimes we want to just stay there. Sometimes we do not have the energy for the spiritual.

Simplifying our lives

- We are lost in our lives, our lives are lost in us. How to make sense, how to find the way?

- Let us annually take an inventory of what we believe—our personal credo. What is wrong in the world, what is right, what is the role of the human in all this, what is my role in all this, what is there to wonder about, what is there to be thankful for?

- Sometimes we come to what we wish could be changed in our lives and we cannot change it because there is a scab or a scar tissue, something dead, in the way. We can go beyond the dead, or enliven it, to the sore tender part inside.

- Where is your source of power? Just as a plug has hidden wire behind it ....

- We live fragmented existences, yet we know that we should be whole, need to be one with ourselves and others. The questions are whether to try, and then how.

Douglas D. Germann, Sr.

◆ Life needs a gentle hand, a light touch.

◆ Sometimes, after perhaps only a few seconds of thinking, I don't know which thought is interrupting which.

◆ When we feel ourselves getting discouraged, we can remember our feelings are like little children. As adults we know from experience that the feeling will pass and can lead ourselves to take it with equanimity, awaiting better times.

◆ We are like those giant bubbles: we shine and shimmer and are multi-colored, even if no one is looking. Eventually we pop and that can be exhilarating. We can be viewed with wide-eyed wonder.

◆ Our world view equates to our horizon. We do not see all.

◆ Move progressively from individuality to similarity to interconnectedness to interpenetration to coinherence to one. Though they are places on a continuum, you can enter it anywhere, and skip about.

Douglas D. Germann, Sr.

- I will not try to prove, but merely to report to those who are receptive. I will try to make what I serve up more than palatable, to be inviting, tasty, delectable.

- I talk about essential stuff, not merely the important.

- Don't let it slip between your fingers.

- Trust is a verb and a noun. Life is a verb and a noun.

- "Suddenly I realized"—have you ever been there? Experienced that? Then you have seen the meaning in life, perhaps glimpsed the divine.

- There is good separation from God and our neighbor and bad. The bad kind says Stay away from me, I'm better than you, I don't know you. The good kind says I'll go out exploring and growing and come back to share what I've found.

Simplifying our lives

- How do you eat popcorn? A whole handful at a time? One kernel per bite? Slathered with butter, loaded with salt? Could it perhaps be a clue to how you live your life?

- I have seen the future, the better world.

- Because we are in life for a long time (eternity), a small change in direction now can make a major difference a few million miles further on.

- The world is not as much oneness as it is allness.

- Is that a political statement on your bumper sticker, or do you believe it?

- I am boundaryless. I seek to be boundaryless.

- Truth is broader and deeper than psychology or any other subdivision of truth.

- Give a gift to someone everyday. It will at least help you realize you are not separate.

- We need some R & R—Receive and respond. Also, we need to listen, imagine, focus. These are paths to truth.

- Just because we cannot know fully does not mean we should give up or deny.

- Spirit is the important stuff of your life—the breath of your life.

- Shrinking is about emotion—stretching is about that and beyond to the thought itself, to everything.

- It is important also to connect with yourself.

- Be bold in truth-telling, fearless. Is this a hint of the meaning of "The truth will set you free"?

- If we are to move from knowledge to wisdom to truth we must move from instruction to experience to emptiness. What therefore is left to teach? What can I teach? Nothing.

- Expand your self-definition and you will live. Who are you? Who are you not? Why? Apply a little what-iffery to yourself and see whom you might be. You are more than you are. Remove one little limit on your self definition and I promise you you will live, you will fly.

- We are each authentic because we have our reasons for being: we are no accidents.

- We need to bring our inner-most out to be true to ourselves.

- There are two kinds of fear—the fear of good and the fear of evil. We dare not treat them the same. We tremble toward one and defy the other.

- Wholeness and chaos are part of each other, but the greater is wholeness.

- Coming from deep, people will write and speak more effectively, persuasively. They will do so because they connect better.

- Anger is positive, good, when it reveals to us the separation in each of us and leads us toward a fusing back. Yet anger is unpleasant, hurts us more than the other, unless we see its pretty side. Anger is OK, temper is not.

- This is life—don't delay.

- If your anger is stifled, it cannot tell its good.

- Why aren't you what you want to be when you grow up?

- When we go into an ethnic restaurant and try to pronounce the words "their way," we are being spiritual: language and words are central to how people think, relate, see themselves and the universe. So trying to get our tongues around their words is a way to connect, to see the world as they do, to hug their words and thoughts and them.

- What really makes us as a people tick?

- Life is fun.

Simplifying our lives

- Anger stems from fear. Fear that we can't have our way if the others get theirs. Fear denies the multiplicity of the universe and its good intent. Anger points at our presumed limits and says "This is where you don't see."

- Why do we kick off our shoes in the presence of the holy? Perhaps so we can be in closer contact.

- Get clear about yourself. Clear the air. Clear fluid is pure, powerful, undilute.

- Solid earth is not solid, immovable. It is in fact a ball floating in space, held in place not just by gravitational forces, but by the interplay of several different gravitational forces. It may be bouncing around not unlike the pinball planets in the opening scenes of the TV show, "Third Rock."

- Real people hug.

- When we seek to get the rights right, eventually we have to speak of truth and ultimacies.

- As the stream is not the same one day to the next as new waters enter and old leave, so we are not the same people each day as new thoughts and experiences enter our lives. Nor are the people with whom we come in contact every day: we must meet them anew in some way each day.

- There are ways to leave a better legacy, but I cannot tell you what they are. The better legacy is you—a piece of yourself. I can tell you how others have done it, and how others are doing it today, some consciously, some not. But I can't give you your own way. You know what it is.

- To let your senses sing, get in touch with reality.

- Internal self speaks to internal self.

- If I write it, it's true. For me. For now.

- Enough already!

- Sound comes from movement. Nothing else.

- The mind is the engine that runs the body-brain. It must be kept tuned up. For this reason we exercise it.

- We should not keep our gifts in boxes. Rather keep them out in the open where they can be shared and do their good.

Douglas D. Germann, Sr.

- Keep a three ring binder where you record for the benefit of your survivors, as you think of these things, what life is for and about. This can be your legacy.

- People come to consciousness from many roads, among others the four traditional paths: positive, negative, creative, transformative.

- We are the flowers on the stem of God.

- Each of us has thoughts—do you agree? And those thoughts bubble up from some boiling, roiling, huge pot called the mind. How did they get in the mind? Some the mind made from its collection of other thoughts. But where did the collection come from? They bubbled through, some from the sides of the pot, some from deeper. How deep can you go? Deeper is truer. Deeper eventually gets to just plain mind—not yours or mine but the thing that underlies all life, all things. That's where we connect with each and all.

- You are simply divine.

- What are the traits which define spirituality to you?

- Why did someone die? How have we managed to get past our mourning? We cannot say. That is the point. Life and love will out.

- Is there intelligent life on earth? Is wisdom a part of intelligence? Is there wisdom among humans?

- Life is a bowl of oatmeal with raisins.

- Use the constant chatter of your mind. Direct it. Listen to it. Ride it. Pay attention. Choose.

- One of our biggest tasks is to resolve the apparent difference between the inner and the outer worlds, between the way it ought to be and the way it is.

- No one can tell you what you should do or not; no one can give you permission. Ultimately, only you can.

- Is sane someplace you start, or someplace you work towards?

- Integrity means to be one with yourself, with others, with truth, with all that is.

- In human times there seem to be no forever changes we can make to our lives. We must be watchful.

- Just as the body gathers the nutrients it needs from the food it is fed, so too we draw the message we need from the stories we hear.

- The difficulty in trying to remove gender references from everyday English is perhaps exacerbated by speaking from a third person perspective, and reduced by being personal.

- How can we connect with people we can barely see, such as through a tinted window on a car? Wave. Open yourself. Reveal yourself. *Namasté*. See with the inner eye, listen with your eyes.

- The big advantage of the fragmentation of life is that it takes our minds off deeper things. Thus it is difficult to break people's preoccupations with fragmentation.

- Why the recent popularity of Bed and Breakfast Inns? Perhaps it is because we savor friendliness and connection in our otherwise lonely travels through this life.

- Life is a struggle, but not a battle. It is a working toward not against. Even the struggle is only within ourselves, not with the outside. All is in more than harmony: all is love, all is one. Life is a releasing, a freedom, a soaring, an acceptance of the soaring.

- In this life we are given to constantly strive for more connection. For if we think we are connected, we stop trying, and we lose our connections.

- Often what we see as evil is an unfamiliar part of us that we fear. When we get to know it, it can combine with the good to expand and grow us in good ways.

- Life bubbles and boils. Life overflows. Life touches life. Life creates life. Life percolates. Life chain reacts.

- I doubt if we can ever get to self mastery. Can we ever know ourselves? But we can attain self-exploration every day.

- Mothers don't want their children to fall. Fathers don't want their children to fail. Would this world move farther, faster, if these parental urges were consciously controlled, more moderately used?

- You have it within you to have an habitual vision of greatness.

- Understand. The meaning of it all!

- There is something more on which to build our lives, and that something more is planted on the inside, the deep side.

- Live life at your fingertips.

Simplifying our lives

- Being complete means taking away the things that crust over us, our illusions. Freedom stems from wholeness, haleness.

- Pray your life.

- We do not know where others are. But we can do better ourselves, raise ourselves. In so doing, we raise all.

- We seek to understand others from within.

- Grow or die.

- We can always do better. Don't accept "You did your best." Do good instead.

- You don't need to grab, it will be given.

- What color are quarks and other elemental things?

- We break through to other people not from the outside, but through the inner tunnel.

- As we grow to realize what life is about, we need more sacred hours, less profane.

- The inside is the reality of us.

- Try seeing: the divine in the ordinary; the extraordinary in the ordinary.

- We are on a stream, floating though the divine. Sometimes we paddle, others rest and enjoy. We will eventually make it to the sea.

- Love, love, every*here*.

- It takes little things and big things to keep love growing—notes with sweet nothings, reminders of love and to love, and listening, the biggest act of love.

- Some of the problem is that we humans have placed so much baggage on our words. Simplify. Use poor words.

- This is a great, and wonderful world.

- The male gives; the female receives. In receiving we give, in giving receive.

- I don't want to add tasks to your load, but to show you through some momentary experiences how to free yourself, your real self, from whatever holds you back.

- Mind and body are connected, else why would we get crotchety when tired?

- Freedom is part of love.

- Few words have color and depth while life has both. Words are inadequate to capture life; words can only point to where it was.

- Boundaries melt. If we take one dissimilarity and look at it long enough, touch it, poke and prod it, perhaps even analyze (gasp!) it, we will see its hardness turn first to liquid, then to vapor, then blow away in the wind. What we thought was separation turns out to be mirage.

Douglas D. Germann, Sr.

Simplifying our lives

- Tormenting ourselves over a question helps the process of internalizing the answer. Without roughing up the surface, the glue doesn't stick.

- Life is not so much web as tapestry.

- Is there something, some cause say, larger than yourself? Is there something you can imagine bigger than anything else? This is what I mean by God. Different for each, bigger than all.

- Perhaps our bodies and minds seek less a general slowing down than a matching of activity to internal rhythms. And perhaps we generally do try to go faster than these rhythms.

- That sloth and evil prospers people more than industry and good is an illusion.

- There is meditation and there is spiritual meditation. You may choose. One has more effects than the other.

- We owe each other life.

- Separation can be a matter of lack of trust, openness, vulnerability: in a phrase, trying to build a hard shell. Softer is more loving, more lovable, more real.

- Get less logical. Logical pens us within a set of rules and laws about what is logical. We need to jump the fence and run free, to stretch. We can do more inside the fence when we get back.

- Anger = tumult = chaos = growth.

- We are called to life—to this life, to our life.

- Sacrifice means giving all.

- Be bold in your humility, through your humility.

- I will be gentle, understanding, open. I will try to emulate what I teach, and teach what I believe.

- It is seldom necessary to work through long lists of questions to find our purpose, our center. We need pick only the one that catches our attention and work on that. We need remind ourselves that the work might proceed unconsciously.

- We need to drop our line where we are instead of trolling along the surface.

- In the funeral of Princess Diana was there more going on than met the eye? More than a silent cortege on a city street with millions lining the streets? Why were they silent? More is soul, more is spirit, more is God.

- We are each of us two or more: we wish to run free, but we want to pay the bills; we want to let our insides express themselves, but we fear what others may think. All parts are us as much as there are weird people and boring, normal and simply odd. It truly takes (and probably needs) all kinds to make a flourishing universe. Give all of you expression, not just part, if you wish to live fully.

- What is your dream? Don't just dream, but dream for something. Martin Luther King, Jr. had a dream for something specific. I dream that others will live lives full and deep. The time has come to bring spirit back into our lives.

- Truth is neither objective, outside of us, nor subjective, inside of us. Truth is.

- If you explore yourself, what will you find? Will it be dark, ugly, putrid, shameful? Or if you peel the layers away is it just as possible that there is something bright, shimmering, living, and pulsing, deep within?

- Our job as humans is to learn to let go of our boundaries. We are constantly striving to live beyond. Yet we cling to our boundaries as if they were life itself. We are not our boundaries. We have created most of our boundaries. We can create bigger ones or take them down as if fences, at any time. Or we can wait till we die and live only partially till then.

- It is your heart which is the gift. The ribbons and the box are mere packaging. Get it out, however imperfect, for whatever good it can do. Don't withhold. It will grow better by sharing and giving. Holding it in hurts us all, because we can't build upon your gift. Giving expands.

- What bigger life are you a part of?

- Life is a living organism: it grows, it withers, it flourishes, it seeds, it dies, it sprouts again. Life if you want it must be watered, fed, encouraged, trimmed, harvested.

- The goal of morning pages is to get to the other side. We do not see that there is anything in between. It is an invisible but very real blockade.

- There is more depth to what is real than the physical. Things have deeper meaning, more wisdom than we at first imagine. This is the burning truth we need to bring to others.

Douglas D. Germann, Sr.

- Living the life you want is your moral duty because any other life is not yours and therefore a lie. So? Living a lie denies your fellows the benefit of your best, your fullest creativity, your furthering of the common life.

Rounding out our lives

What does it mean to simplify our lives? We want to boil down our lives to the essence, to what is most real about us.

We feel frazzled and pulled in all directions. There is so much going on in our lives. Spouses and children and parents all demand pieces of us. Bosses and customers and clients and volunteer opportunities overrun our time. When is there time for me? We want to simmer away all the excess and live simply, to be simply us.

And yet we resonate to the call to add more gusto to our lives, to live more fully. We don't want to miss a thing.

Is there a way to do both?

It is not a matter of balancing things, it is a matter of being whole.

It is not, as some will suppose, a matter of controlling our lives, for we cannot control what is bigger than us. Life is a mystery. We cannot plan out our lives decades ahead and say on June 12th, 11 years from now I will be sitting at my desk writing my 6th best seller. How boring! We would not want to live a pre-plotted life.

Again, it is fullness that matters, not cutting things out. When we try to simplify, we are saying things are sticking out of our lives, and we cannot make them fit.

Where do these poking out parts come from? From not having a bigger picture of our lives. How do we fit in the web of all life? For just as planets orbit stars and subatomic particles orbit other subatomic particles, smaller things are a part of us, and we are part of a larger life than just our own.

Once we see how we fit, even if dimly, we can draw a larger circle around our lives, make poking pieces fit, discard the unessential—the dead and deadening parts—and free ourselves to fly, to have it all.

What is this "it?" Ah, it is the essential us, the part which is of all and all is of it. You are more than you are. "Know yourself," said the ancients. Such an easy, hard thing to do. Once you start on this path, you know where to draw the circle. And it is a bigger circle than either of us can know.

So start.

About the author

Douglas D. Germann, Sr. has been in business for over 25 years, and has over 50 years' experience at life.

Doug heads up four entrepreneurial ventures: a legal practice; a publishing and speaking company; and two real estate rental operations. He has worked for a Fortune 500 company, and as an attorney and CPA.

He is married, and has (most days) the two smartest children in the world. Doug's real life's work is fishing.

Doug is a member of the National Speakers Association, and was twice elected president of the state chapter in Indiana.

If you would like to ask Doug questions or share your own insights, you may reach him at 415 Lincoln Way West, Mishawaka, IN 46544, telephone 219/255-0022, fax 219/255-0024, or e-mail 76066.515@CompuServe.com.

Doug is also available to come to your group for a presentation or workshop on the subject of any of his books.

Simplifying our lives

Special thanks to:

Linda Germann, who has put up with my constantly being in front of the computer.

Joanne Hill, Marie Leddy, and Barbara Steele whose many suggestions improved immensely the final product you see here.

Judd Lowenhar and Ginger Taylor, from Duley Press, who have nursed me through the tough days.

Order blank

Please send me

#	Title	Each	Total
	◆ Contraplanned: Contrarian insights on goal-setting, planning, and success	10.97	
	◆ Simplifying our lives: Insights to living fully now	10.97	
	◆ Leaping through flames: Insights for leaders	10.97	
	◆ Beyond Dollars and Numbers: Insights on business, work, and money	10.97	
	◆ Beyond creativity: Insights on daring, discovery and dreamsmithing	10.97	
	◆ How to get to happy from here: The happiness insights	10.97	
	◆ Everyday Awe: Insights to the divine at work and play	10.97	
	◆ Buying a Business (For Very Little Cash)	21.95	
	Shipping and handling per book	2.00	

Total order (cash, check ,credit cards)

Charge to Visa Mastercard #_____ exp:_____
Name_____
Address_____
_____
City _____ State ___ Zip_____

Mail orders to (please ask about bulk discounts):
Learning Works, Incorporated
415 Lincoln Way West
Mishawaka, IN 46544
Or fax to: 219/255-0024

Simplifying our lives   99

Order blank

Please send me

#	Title	Each	Total
	• Contraplanned: Contrarian insights on goal-setting, planning, and success	10.97	
	• Simplifying our lives: Insights to living fully now	10.97	
	• Leaping through flames: Insights for leaders	10.97	
	• Beyond Dollars and Numbers: Insights on business, work, and money	10.97	
	• Beyond creativity: Insights on daring, discovery and dreamsmithing	10.97	
	• How to get to happy from here: The happiness insights	10.97	
	• Everyday Awe: Insights to the divine at work and play	10.97	
	• Buying a Business (For Very Little Cash)	21.95	
	Shipping and handling per book	2.00	

Total order (cash, check ,credit cards)

Charge to Visa Mastercard #_____ exp:____
Name_____
Address_____
_____
City _____ State ___ Zip____

Mail orders to (please ask about bulk discounts):
Learning Works, Incorporated
415 Lincoln Way West
Mishawaka, IN 46544
Or fax to: 219/255-0024